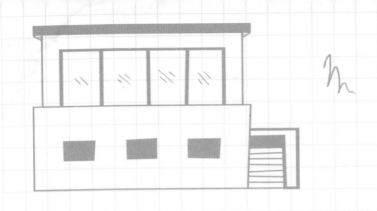

ARCHITECT
ACADEMY

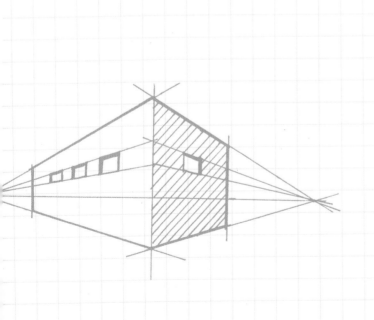

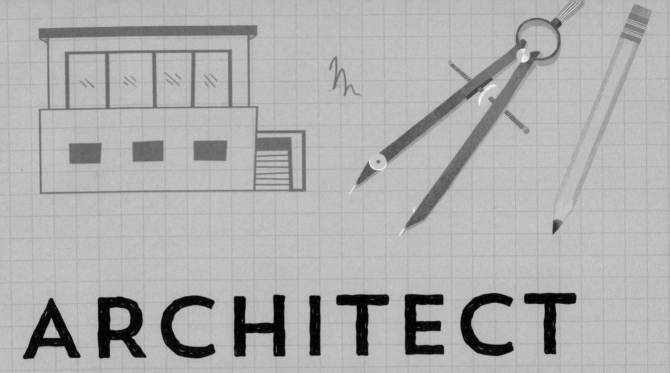

ARCHITECT
ACADEMY

WRITTEN BY
STEVE MARTIN

ILLUSTRATED BY
ESSI KIMPIMÄKI

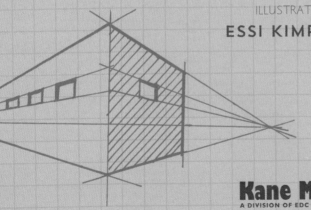

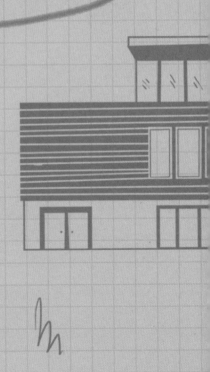

Kane Miller
A DIVISION OF EDC PUBLISHING

CONTENTS

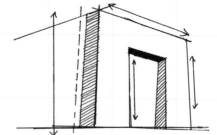

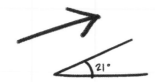

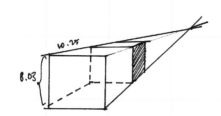

BUILDINGS

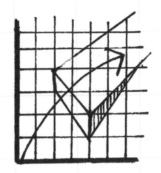

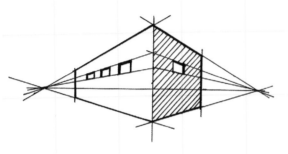

SPECIALIST ARCHITECTURE

ARCHITECT GOODIES

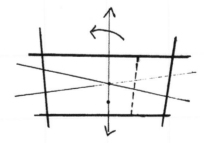

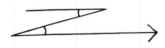

WELCOME TO ARCHITECT ACADEMY!

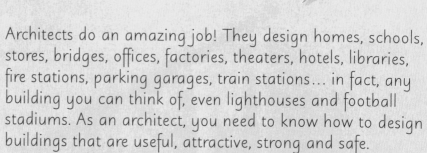

Architects do an amazing job! They design homes, schools, stores, bridges, offices, factories, theaters, hotels, libraries, fire stations, parking garages, train stations… in fact, any building you can think of, even lighthouses and football stadiums. As an architect, you need to know how to design buildings that are useful, attractive, strong and safe.

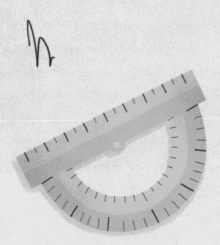

The buildings you design may cost millions of dollars to build. People may live, learn, work or play in them. You might even be designing a building that will be there for hundreds of years! This is why you need to develop your architectural skills to the highest standard.

At the Academy, you will gain the skills and knowledge you need. These include:

- Learning about famous buildings
- Creating designs for buildings
- Understanding how buildings are constructed
- Learning about different types of buildings
- Developing the math skills architects need
- Carrying out special projects, such as designing ships and parks

Your first task is to fill in your Trainee Architect ID Card.

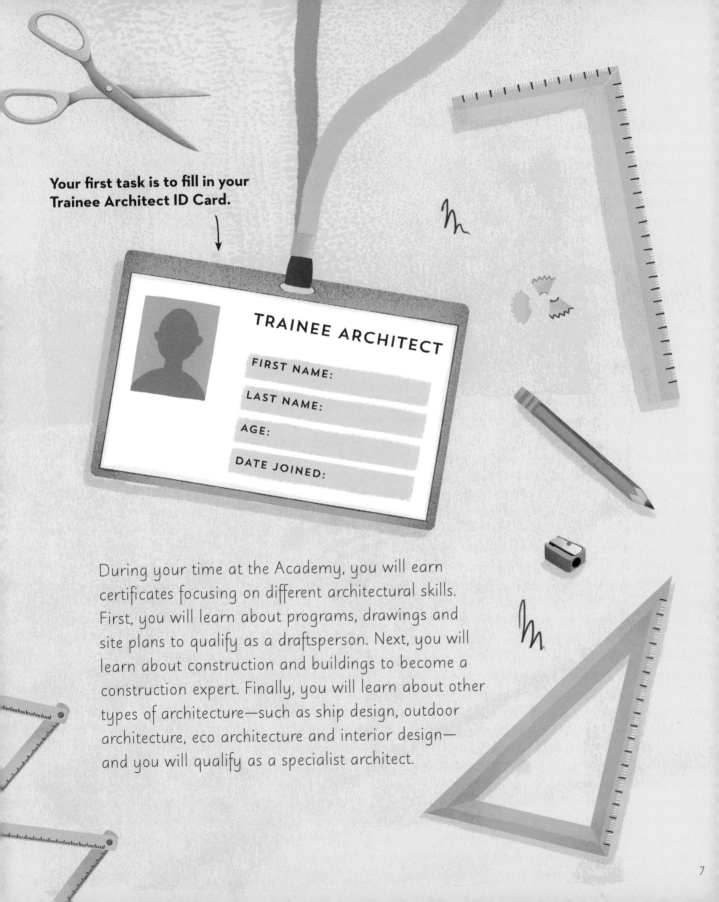

TRAINEE ARCHITECT

FIRST NAME:

LAST NAME:

AGE:

DATE JOINED:

During your time at the Academy, you will earn certificates focusing on different architectural skills. First, you will learn about programs, drawings and site plans to qualify as a draftsperson. Next, you will learn about construction and buildings to become a construction expert. Finally, you will learn about other types of architecture—such as ship design, outdoor architecture, eco architecture and interior design— and you will qualify as a specialist architect.

LEARNING FROM THE BEST

SIX FAMOUS HISTORICAL BUILDINGS

If you study famous buildings, you'll be learning from the best! People have been designing structures for thousands of years and there are many incredible buildings in Europe, Africa, Asia and the Americas that have lasted many centuries. Here you can learn about six very old, famous buildings, all of which can still be visited today.

FIND THE MATCH

The pictures and their information have been mixed up. Can you sort them out? Read the descriptions and then write the correct letter in the white circle next to the matching picture.

We've done the first one for you.

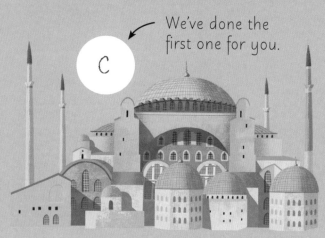

C

A The Parthenon, in the Greek city of Athens, was built more than 2,500 years ago as a temple to the goddess Athena. The temple has a series of 46 columns around the outside.

E The pyramids of Giza, in Egypt, are more than 4,500 years old. The largest, the Great Pyramid, is made from 2.3 million blocks of stone and weighs nearly six million tons!

F The Colosseum was a huge stadium in Rome, built by the Romans in the 1st century. It held 50,000 people who came to watch the bloodthirsty gladiator contests. A series of arches surround three of the stories.

D The Taj Mahal, in Agra, India, was built in the 17th century by a grieving emperor in memory of his dead wife. The building, with its 240-foot-high dome, took 20,000 workmen more than 20 years to finish.

C The Hagia Sophia, in Istanbul, Turkey, has an enormous dome. Underneath the dome, a circle of 40 windows floods the building with light. It was built in the 6th century as a cathedral.

B Chichen Itza, in Mexico, was a city built by the Mayans between the eighth and twelfth centuries. One of the main buildings is a pyramid called El Castillo. Each of its four sides has 91 stairs. The top step makes a total of 365 steps—the same number as the number of days in a year.

Check your answers below, then place your sticker here. →

PLACE STICKER HERE

TASK COMPLETE

— SIX FAMOUS —
MODERN BUILDINGS

On these pages you can discover six famous modern buildings.

Completed in 2012, the 1,000-foot-high, 87-story Shard soars above the London skyline. It was designed by architect Renzo Piano and its pointed shape was inspired by the city's church spires.

Sydney Opera House was designed by Jørn Utzon and completed in 1973. It is Australia's most famous building. Located in Sydney Harbour, its roof design looks like the sails of the boats that pass by.

Work started on La Sagrada Familia Cathedral in Barcelona, Spain, in 1882 and still isn't finished! This huge church can hold 13,000 people. Its architect, Antoni Gaudí, was inspired by medieval church architecture.

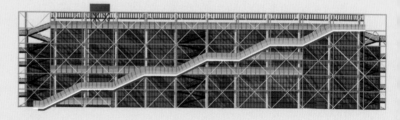

The Pompidou Centre in Paris opened in 1977. It looks more like a building from a science fiction film than an art gallery. It was designed by architects Renzo Piano and Richard Rogers.

New York City's Empire State Building, completed in 1931, was the world's tallest building for more than 40 years. It was the first building ever to have more than 100 floors. The tip of its antenna spire is more than ¼ mile from the ground! The architect was William F. Lamb.

The Guggenheim Museum in New York City was constructed in 1959 and designed by architect Frank Lloyd Wright. Built in circles, and growing wider as it gets higher, it looks as if an alien spacecraft has landed in the middle of the city.

DESIGN A NEW EMPIRE STATE BUILDING

Here is the base of the Empire State Building. Finish it off, but make it look completely different than the original!

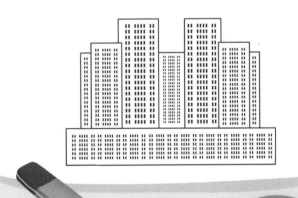

When you have finished your design for the Empire State Building, place your sticker here.

PLACE STICKER HERE

TASK COMPLETE

THE PROGRAM

The work of an architect starts with the "program." This is a set of instructions written by the person who owns or is paying for the building, who is called the "client." Look at this example of a brief for the new home of a movie star.

OUR NEW HOME

- It must look very modern and bright.
- There should be plenty of large windows to let in lots of light.
- There should be at least four bedrooms as I often have friends stay over.
- The kitchen and dining room should be joined together. This should be a large room that is able to seat at least ten of my friends around the dining table.
- I will need a home theater for watching movies, with enough space for a large screen.
- I will need a study for reading movie scripts and e-mails.
- I will need a garage large enough for my two cars.
- I will need a gym for working out.
- Since I am away a lot filming, the yard should be small and easy to look after, perhaps with paving instead of a lawn.

WRITE A PROGRAM FOR YOUR DREAM HOME

You are now going to complete a program for your own dream home. Here are some ideas to think about to help you write it.

- What design style do you prefer—traditional or modern?
- Would you like a house or an apartment?
- How many bedrooms will you need?
- What special rooms would you like? A game room, a home theater, an indoor swimming pool?

- How would you like to get from room to room—by stairs, elevator, slide or tunnel?
- Would you like a roof terrace or a balcony?
- What would you like outside? A big yard with a soccer field, an adventure playground, a tree house?

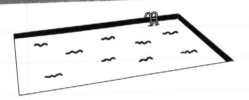

MY DREAM HOME

PLACE STICKER HERE

When you have completed the program, place your sticker here.

TASK COMPLETE

FLOOR PLANS

Architects have different ways of drawing buildings. One method is to draw floor plans. These show the entire layout of each floor of a building, including the rooms, doors and hallways, as well as bathrooms. They are drawn as if looking down from above.

This drawing shows the floor plan of an apartment. The key below shows what the different lines and shapes mean.

FRONT DOOR

KITCHEN

LIVING ROOM

DINING ROOM

CLOSET

BEDROOM 1

BATHROOM

BEDROOM 2

BEDROOM 3

KEY

———— outside wall

———— inside wall

———— window

door

sink

bathtub

toilet

FINISH OFF A FLOOR PLAN

On the plan below, choose which rooms will be the bedroom, bathroom, living room and kitchen. Using the symbols shown opposite, draw the positions of the doors, toilet, bathtub and sink.

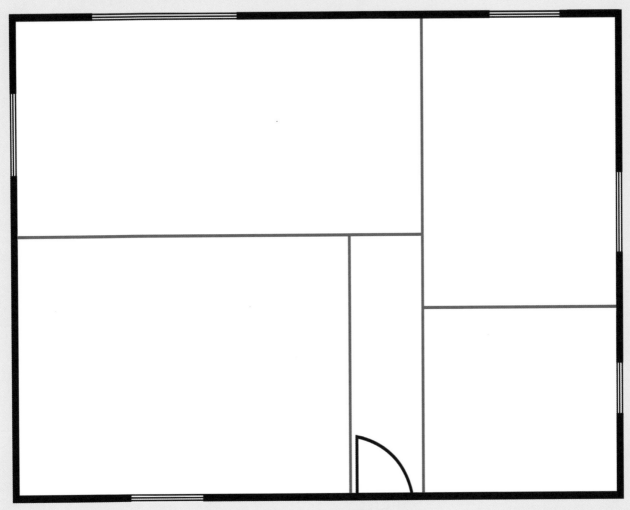

FRONT
DOOR

When you have drawn your floor plan, place your sticker here.

PLACE
STICKER
HERE

TASK COMPLETE

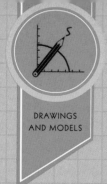

HOW TO BUILD A
MODEL HOUSE

Architects must be able to transform their flat building plans into a three-dimensional (3-D) model. This shows them how a building will look once it's built.

MAKE A 3-D MODEL

You will need: card stock, scissors, a ruler, a pencil, colored markers, glue or adhesive tape

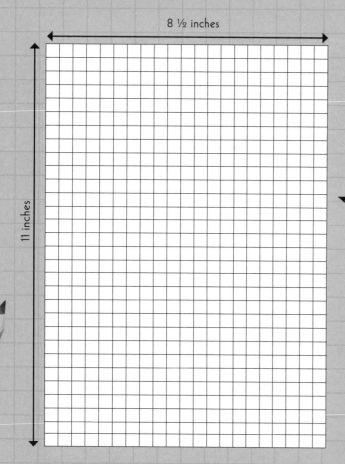

8 ½ inches

11 inches

1. Use a sheet of card stock, 8 ½ inches wide and 11 inches long.
2. Use the ruler to measure and draw lines across the card, spaced ¼ inch apart.
3. Draw lines down the card, spaced ¼ inch apart.

4. Copy the diagram on the opposite page onto your card. The grid lines are shown to help you. Color it in.
5. Cut the shape out along the outside edges. You can see these in red on the plan.
6. Fold along the lines shown in blue on the plan.
7. Glue or tape the model together, following the yellow "glue" tabs. Bend the tabs so they fit behind a wall before you glue them.

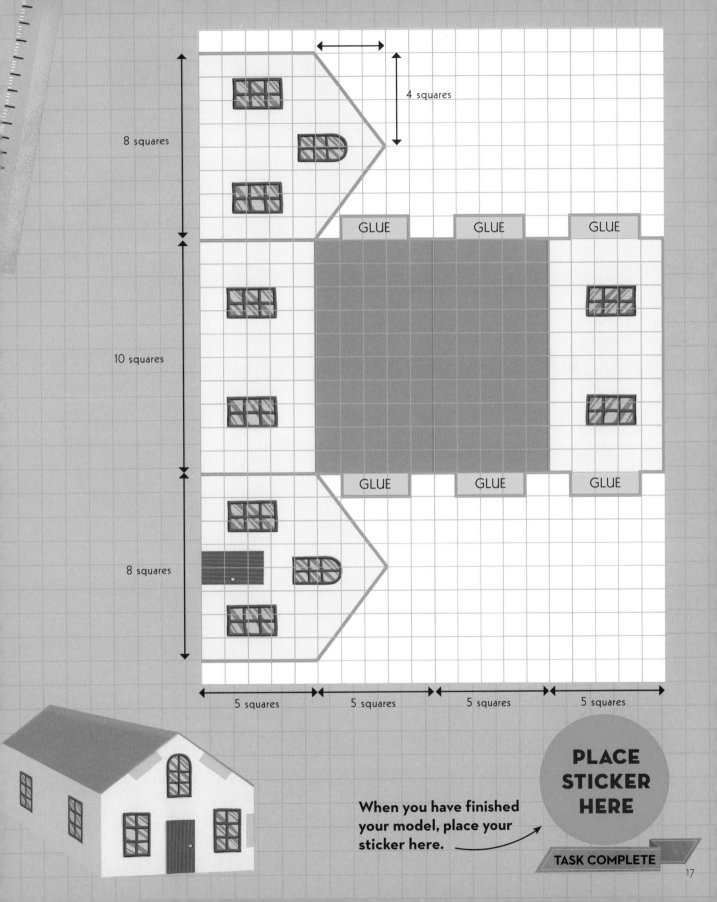

8 squares

4 squares

10 squares

8 squares

GLUE   GLUE   GLUE

GLUE   GLUE   GLUE

5 squares   5 squares   5 squares   5 squares

When you have finished your model, place your sticker here.

PLACE STICKER HERE

TASK COMPLETE

17

SITE PLANS

An architect might have to plan an entire neighborhood. Imagine you are in an airplane flying over a residential (housing) area. It might look something like the drawing below. The white blocks are homes, the white lines are roads and the green areas are grass.

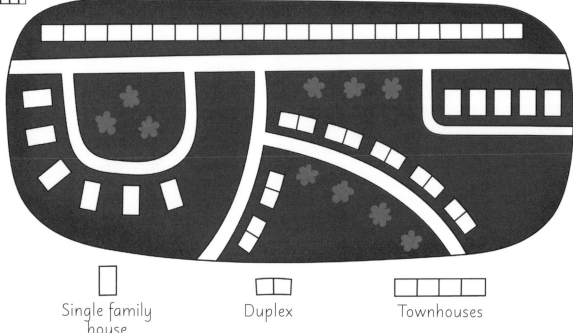

Single family house

Duplex

Townhouses

**This is how an architect plans a residential development.
There are a number of things they must think about when planning:**

- The architect needs to fit a lot of homes into the area.
  The plan above has 47 building lots (pieces of land).
- It must also be a pleasant area to live in, so the design should include green spaces (grass areas) and maybe trees and flower beds.
- Every building must be next to a road, so that people can reach it.
- Usually, the architect will include a mix of home types. In the plan above, there is a row of townhouses, as well as some single family homes, and some duplexes.

DESIGN A RESIDENTIAL DEVELOPMENT

Now, it's your turn! Use the grid below to plan a neighborhood of houses. You need to include a mix of single family homes, duplexes and townhouses. Single family homes should be 2 squares long and 1 square wide. Duplexes and townhouses should each be 1 square.

Every house should be next to a road. A road has been drawn in to start you off, but you can add more.

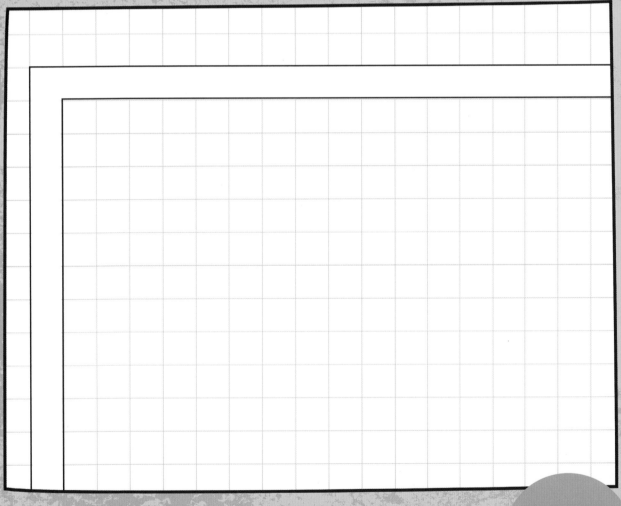

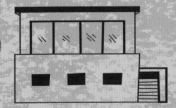

When you have finished your plan, place your sticker here. →

PLACE STICKER HERE

TASK COMPLETE

DRAWING TO SCALE

In a scale drawing, all the measurements are reduced by exactly the same amount. For example, if every measurement of a building was 100 times smaller in the drawing, the scale would be "1 to 100"—this is usually written as 1:100.

MEASURE A SCALE DRAWING

In this scale drawing of a floor plan, every 1 square represents 16 feet. This means if a building is 80 feet long, it will be 5 squares long on this grid, because 16 x 5 = 80. Can you write the correct measurements in feet in the white boxes?

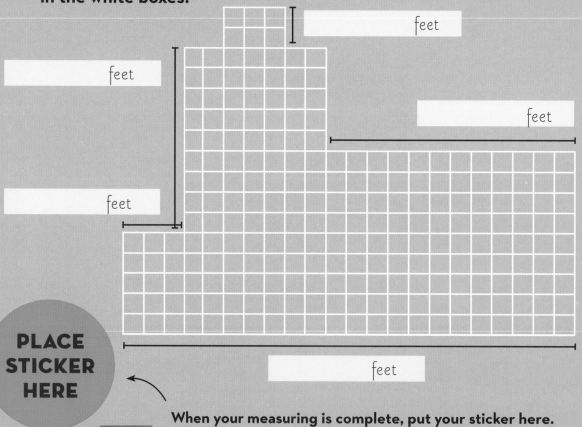

feet

feet

feet

feet

feet

PLACE STICKER HERE

When your measuring is complete, put your sticker here.

TASK COMPLETE

ANSWERS (from top to bottom): 32 ft., 144 ft., 192 ft., 48 ft., 352 ft.

20

Congratulations! You are now a...

— QUALIFIED —
DRAFTSPERSON

NAME: -

The above-named architect
is qualified to be a
DRAFTSPERSON.

Architect Academy would like
to wish you every success
in your new career.

GOOD LUCK!

QUALIFICATION DATE: -

MEASURING

An architect needs to understand measurements to be able to calculate the correct sizes in buildings. The most important tool for measuring is the tape measure.

Measurements are taken in inches (in.), feet (ft.) and yards (yd.).

Can you answer the questions below? The answers are at the bottom of the page.

_____ in. = 1 ft.   _____ ft. = 1 yd.

Ask someone to measure your height with a tape measure and record this below. You will be somewhere between 1 yard and 2 yards tall.

I am _____ ft. and _____ in. tall.

Now measure the other person's height.

_____ is _____ ft. and _____ in. tall.

ANSWERS: 12 in. = 1 ft.; 3 ft. = 1 yd.

MEASURE YOUR THROWS

You are going to practice measuring.

You will need:

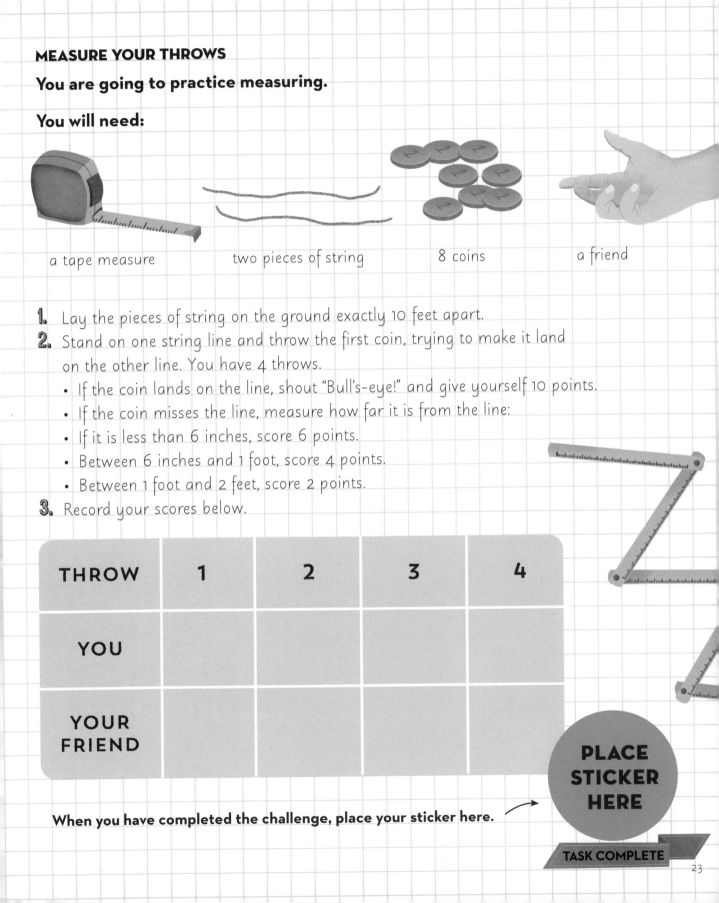

a tape measure   two pieces of string   8 coins   a friend

1. Lay the pieces of string on the ground exactly 10 feet apart.
2. Stand on one string line and throw the first coin, trying to make it land on the other line. You have 4 throws.
   - If the coin lands on the line, shout "Bull's-eye!" and give yourself 10 points.
   - If the coin misses the line, measure how far it is from the line:
   - If it is less than 6 inches, score 6 points.
   - Between 6 inches and 1 foot, score 4 points.
   - Between 1 foot and 2 feet, score 2 points.
3. Record your scores below.

THROW	1	2	3	4
YOU				
YOUR FRIEND				

When you have completed the challenge, place your sticker here.

PLACE STICKER HERE

TASK COMPLETE

23

AREA AND PERIMETER

Two useful measuring terms for architects are "area" and "perimeter." Area is the space covered by the floor—so if a floor is covered by a carpet, the amount of carpet is the area. Perimeter is the lengths of all the sides added together. If there was a wall around a field, its entire length would be the field's perimeter.

COLOR IN HARRY

Color in this grid to meet Harry, the Robot Architect. Nobody understands math as well as a robot! Harry is going to help explain "area" and "perimeter."

Following the key below, color in each square of the grid with a letter in it:

R = Red
Y = Yellow
O = Orange
B = Blue
G = Gray

					B	B	B	B	B				
					B	Y	B	Y	B				
					B	B	B	B	B				
					B	G	G	G	B				
							B						
							B						
					B	B	B	B	B				
	O	G	G	G	B	R	R	R	B	G	G	G	O
	O	G	G	G	B	R	R	R	B	G	G	G	O
					B	R	R	R	B				
					B	R	R	R	B				
					B	R	R	R	B				
					B	R	R	R	B				
					B	B	B	B	B				
					G	G		G	G				
					G	G		G	G				
					G	G		G	G				
					G	G		G	G				
					G	G		G	G				
					G	G		G	G				
					O	O		O	O				

PERIMETER

If you count the squares all the way around Harry's head, there are 14. The distance around the edge of a shape is the "perimeter."

In exactly the same way, the perimeter of the front of this red building is 14 yards.

1	2	3	4	5
14				6
13				7
12	11	10	9	8

1 yd.	2 yd.	3 yd.	4 yd.	5 yd.
14 yd.				6 yd.
13 yd.				7 yd.
12 yd.	11 yd.	10 yd.	9 yd.	8 yd.

AREA

If you count up all the squares in Harry's "stomach" there are 40. The space covered by a shape like this is the "area."

In exactly the same way, the area of the front of the tall blue building on the right is 40 square yards (written as 40 sq. yd.).

1	2	3	4	5
6	7	8	9	10
11	12	13	14	15
16	17	18	19	20
21	22	23	24	25
26	27	28	29	30
31	32	33	34	35
36	37	38	39	40

1 yd.	2 yd.	3 yd.	4 yd.	5 yd.
6 yd.	7 yd.	8 yd.	9 yd.	10 yd.
11 yd.	12 yd.	13 yd.	14 yd.	15 yd.
16 yd.	17 yd.	18 yd.	19 yd.	20 yd.
21 yd.	22 yd.	23 yd.	24 yd.	25 yd.
26 yd.	27 yd.	28 yd.	29 yd.	30 yd.
31 yd.	32 yd.	33 yd.	34 yd.	35 yd.
36 yd.	37 yd.	38 yd.	39 yd.	40 yd.

A quick way to find the area of a rectangle is to multiply the length by the width. The area of my head is 5 x 4 = 20.

Once you have colored in Harry, place your sticker here.

PLACE STICKER HERE

TASK COMPLETE

BUILDING A —PYRAMID—

The Great Pyramid in Egypt has four sides, each 755.9 feet long. You are going to build your own pyramid. You will need to measure accurately so that all four sides join together neatly at the top!

MAKE A PERFECT PYRAMID

You will need: a piece of card stock, a ruler, a pencil, scissors, colored pencils, tape, glue and sand (optional)

1. Measure and draw a square in the center of the card stock. Each side should be 4 in. Be very careful with your measuring—all the sides must be exactly the same length.

4 in.

4 in.

4 in.

2 in.

2. Measure halfway along one side (2 in.). From here, draw a 4 in. line at a right angle to the side.

3. Draw two lines from the tip of the line to the square, making a triangle.

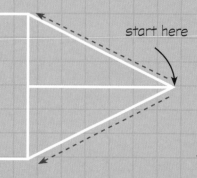

start here

4. Repeat on the other three sides. Remember to start the first line at the center of the side. All the triangles must be the same height.

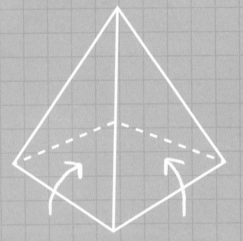

5. Color in your pyramid. Then cut the shape out and fold the triangles upward from the base. If you have measured accurately they will all meet at the top!

6. Tape the triangles together, so that the pyramid stays in shape.

7. If you like, you can cover your pyramid in glue and pour sand over it to make an awesome model!

When you have made the model pyramid, place your sticker here. ➔

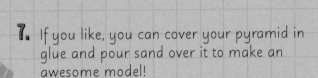

PLACE STICKER HERE

TASK COMPLETE

27

PARTS OF A BUILDING

There are many parts to a building, each doing a different job. As you can see from these two pictures, buildings can have many of the same construction features, even when they look very different!

ROOF
Protects from the weather, insulates (keeps heat in)

WALLS
Enclose the inside, protect from the weather, insulate, hold up the roof

FACADE
The front or face gives the building its character and look.

DOORWAY
Allows people in and out

WINDOWS
Let in light, allow air in

This modern home looks very different from the mud hut on the left, but they share the same construction features.

LABEL THE HOUSE

Add the labels from the hut to this brand-new house. The answers are at the bottom of the page.

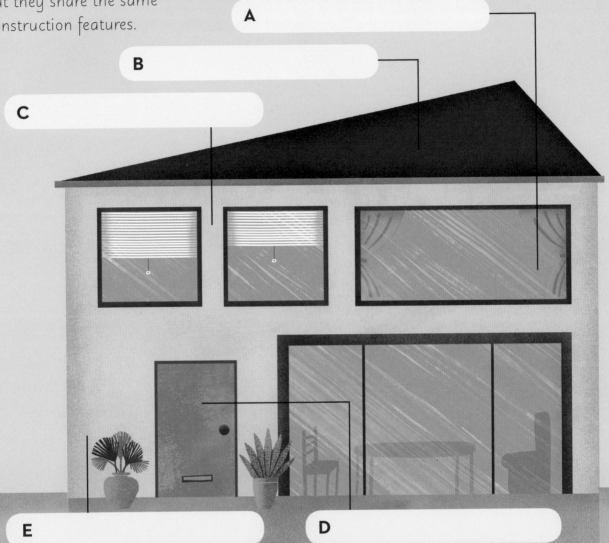

A

B

C

E

D

Both buildings have roofs that slope. The first is made from straw and the second from roof tiles. Before you collect your sticker, you need to answer this question.

Why do the roofs slope?

A To keep birds from building nests on them
B To allow rain water to slide off
C To make the building more stable

When you have labeled the features and answered the question, place your sticker here.

PLACE STICKER HERE

TASK COMPLETE

29

CONSTRUCTION

THE CONSTRUCTION SITE
— WHO DOES WHAT? —

The architect often visits the construction site to check on how work is progressing. The site is a busy place and it is useful to know what everyone is doing. Look at the picture below to see who does what job.

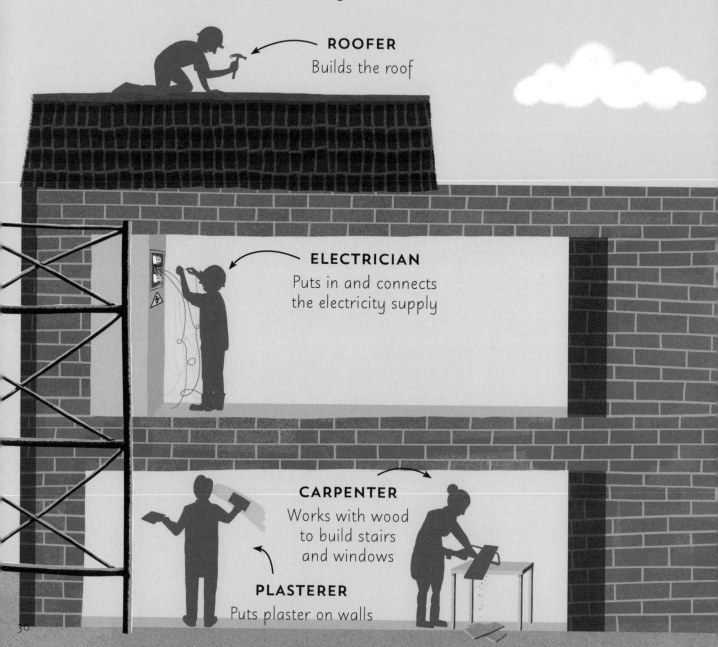

ROOFER
Builds the roof

ELECTRICIAN
Puts in and connects
the electricity supply

CARPENTER
Works with wood
to build stairs
and windows

PLASTERER
Puts plaster on walls

BRICKLAYER
Builds walls

COMPLETE THE PICTURE
Using the stickers at the back of the book, match the correct sticker to the correct worker on the construction site.

PLUMBER
Puts in the water and waste pipes

GLAZIER
Works with glass

PLACE STICKER HERE

PAINTER
ecorates the walls and ceilings

TASK COMPLETE

TYPES OF BUILDING MATERIALS

There are many different types of building materials, each with its own strengths. It is the architect's job to choose the right material for the job.

CONCRETE

As strong as stone and can be poured into different shapes before it gets hard

BRICK

Very strong and can be joined together in a variety of ways to form different shapes

WOOD

Easy to saw, and can be used in lots of different ways

GLASS

Allows in light and protects from the weather

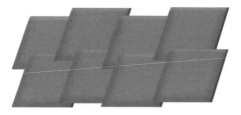

ROOF TILES

Waterproof and usually fitted in overlapping rows

STEEL

One of the strongest of all building materials

WHICH MATERIAL GOES WHERE?

Write the name of the best material for each part of the house next to each letter.

A

B

C

D

E

F

When you have chosen your building materials, place your sticker here.

PLACE STICKER HERE

TASK COMPLETE

CLIMATE

Architects have to design buildings that are suitable for the weather conditions, or climate, of a particular place.

In hot climates, houses are designed to keep cool. Here are some of the ways architects design houses to do this:

- Walls are painted white to reflect the heat.
- Windows face away from the sun.
- Thicker walls help the interior to stay cool.
- Trees, porches and shutters on the windows all give shade.

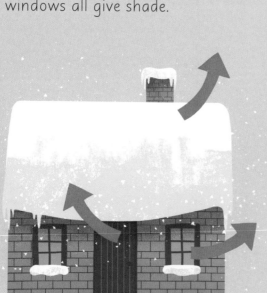

In cold climates, houses need to be insulated to stop heat escaping. Warm air escapes most easily from windows, roofs and doors. Here are some ways architects prevent this:

- Windows are double-glazed so they have two panes of glass instead of one.
- Roofs are lined with thick material.
- Draft excluders around doors keep out cold air.
- Walls are filled with insulating material to keep in heat.

INSULATION EXPERIMENT

In this experiment, you will discover which material— aluminum foil, cotton balls, newspaper or wool—is best at insulating, or keeping in the heat.

You will need: 4 glasses the same size and shape, aluminum foil, cotton balls, newspaper, a wool sock, warm water, 4 rubber bands, a thermometer, an adult to help you

1. Wrap a different material around each glass, leaving enough to overlap at the top.
2. Ask an adult to pour the same amount of warm water into each glass.
3. Cover the top of each glass with the material and secure it with a rubber band.
4. Leave the glasses for 30 minutes, then unwrap the materials.
5. Using the thermometer, test the temperature of the water in each glass.
6. Write down the results in the table below. The higher the temperature, the better the material is at insulating, or keeping in heat. Which was the best insulating material? The answer is at the bottom of the page.

Remember to leave enough material to cover the top of each glass.

MATERIAL	TEMPERATURE AFTER 30 MINUTES
ALUMINUM FOIL	
COTTON BALLS	
NEWSPAPER	
WOOL SOCK	

When you have completed the experiment, place your sticker here.

PLACE STICKER HERE

TASK COMPLETE

ANSWER: The aluminum foil is the best insulator because it reflects the heat back.

PROBLEM SOLVING

An important part of an architect's work is problem solving.

For example, in Hong Kong cars drive on the left-hand side of the road, but in China cars drive on the right. This was a problem for the architects who had to design a road bridge linking Hong Kong to China. How could they stop cars from crashing into each other as they drove over the bridge from their own country?

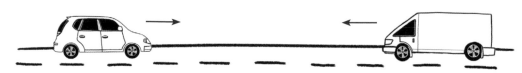

The problem was solved when the architects came up with the idea for the famous "flipper" bridge. This clever design means drivers can cross from one driving system to the other in perfect safety.

Cars coming from China approach the bridge driving on the right-hand side of the road...

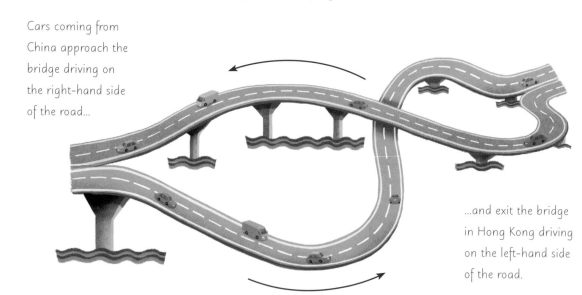

...and exit the bridge in Hong Kong driving on the left-hand side of the road.

Some of the biggest cities in the world, from Tokyo to Los Angeles, are built in areas that can be hit by large earthquakes. Architects need to design buildings that will not collapse when an earthquake strikes. The picture below shows one way to make a building "earthquake proof."

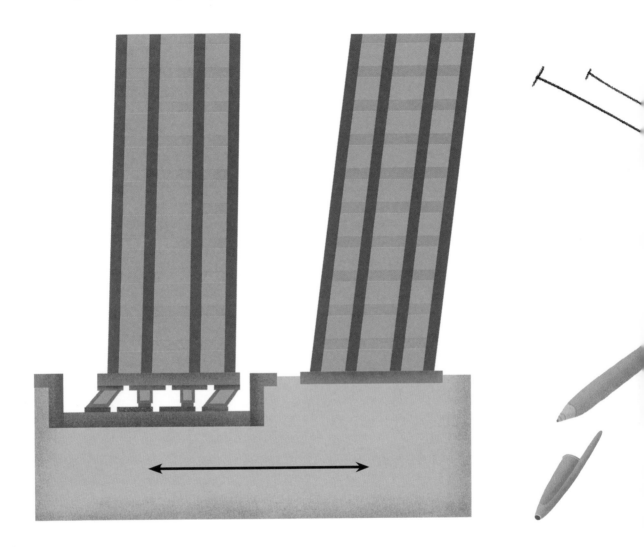

The tower on the left is built on top of giant, spring-like "shock absorbers." When the ground moves in an earthquake, these shock absorbers move with it, keeping the building stable. Architects also use steel frames, which are stronger and lighter than brick or stone walls.

ARCHITECT
INFO

PROBLEM SOLVING—
YOUR TURN

Now it's your turn to solve a problem!

FIT FIVE ROOMS INTO A FLOOR PLAN

Using the gridded floor space on the opposite page, draw the walls of the five rooms listed below. Each room must not be smaller than the size given (though it can be bigger). What is the best way of planning the space? The first room has been done for you.

You will need: a pencil, a ruler, an eraser

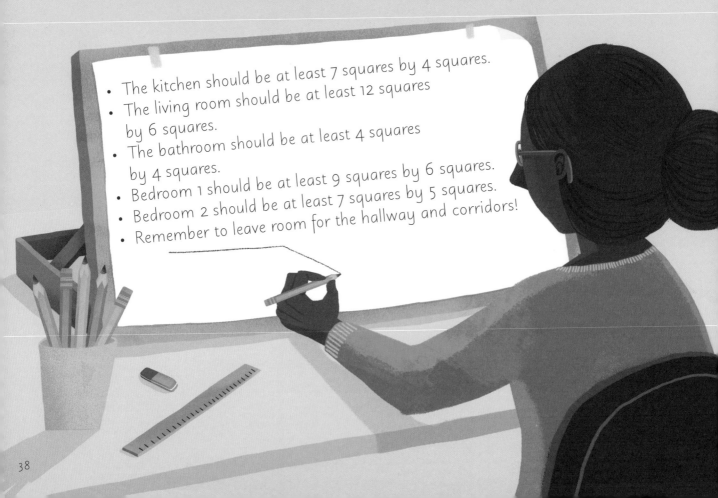

- The kitchen should be at least 7 squares by 4 squares.
- The living room should be at least 12 squares by 6 squares.
- The bathroom should be at least 4 squares by 4 squares.
- Bedroom 1 should be at least 9 squares by 6 squares.
- Bedroom 2 should be at least 7 squares by 5 squares.
- Remember to leave room for the hallway and corridors!

Kitchen

When you have finished, collect your sticker and place it here.

PLACE
STICKER
HERE

TASK COMPLETE

BUILDINGS

HOME, SWEET HOME

There are hundreds of millions of homes around the world, and millions more are built every year. They come in all sorts of shapes and sizes.

BUNGALOW
Popular with older people as there is no need to climb stairs

APARTMENT BUILDING
Used when a lot of people need to live in a small space, they are found in cities around the world

HOUSE ON STILTS
Built near rivers and lakes; the stilts protect the house from flooding

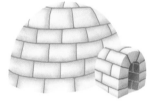

IGLOO
Uses natural resources and is easy to build, with thick walls to keep in the warmth in the freezing Arctic Circle

YURT
Can be taken down and put up quickly somewhere else; useful for nomadic people in Mongolia who move a lot

HOUSEBOAT
Popular with people who love living on the water and close to nature

DESIGN A TREE HOUSE

Another type of home is a tree house! Use this space to design one for you and your friends. You can have as many rooms, levels, ropes, walkways and ladders as you wish.

When you have finished your tree house, place your sticker here.

PLACE STICKER HERE

TASK COMPLETE

STATIONS, STORES AND SCHOOLS

It's not just homes that need architects. There are lots of public buildings that need to be designed, too. These include:

- Hospitals and medical centers
- Fire stations and police stations
- Recreation centers and sports stadiums
- Railroad stations, airports and bus stations
- Shopping malls, storefronts and department stores
- Theaters, libraries, museums and theme parks
- Hotels and restaurants
- Factories and offices
- And, of course… schools!

DESIGN A PLAYGROUND

Your school needs a new adventure playground. Your job is to think of at least five things that the new playground should have. You might include swings, an obstacle course, slides, a trapeze, a fort or a tree house. Draw or label them on the plan below.

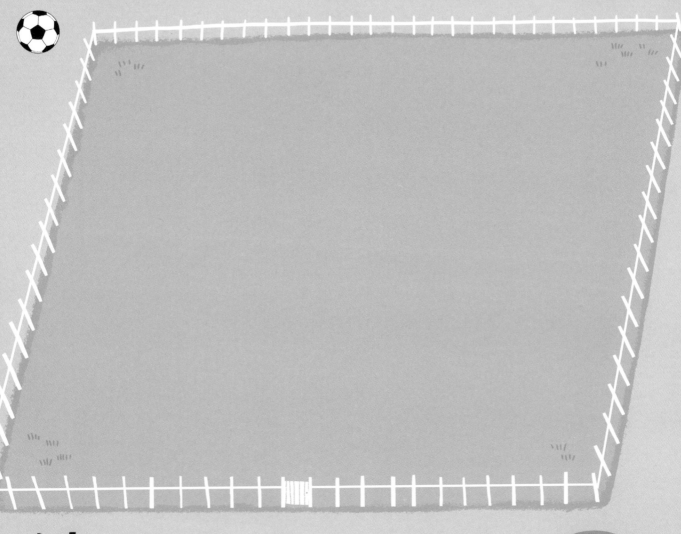

When you have planned the new playground, collect your sticker and put it here.

PLACE STICKER HERE

TASK COMPLETE

BRIDGES

Bridges can be beautiful, and some of them are among the best-loved structures in the world. They need to be carefully designed though, because they have to be very strong. They have to cope with heavy vehicles passing over them every day, and extreme weather such as gale-force winds. Here are some different types of bridges:

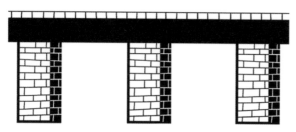

BEAM BRIDGE

Beam bridges are supported at each end by a column—just like a plank of wood set on top of two bricks. Lake Pontchartrain Causeway in Louisiana is a 23-mile-long beam bridge!

SUSPENSION BRIDGE

Suspension bridges, like the Golden Gate Bridge in San Francisco, support the weight of the road with vertical cables suspended from other cables running between towers.

ARCH BRIDGE

The Sydney Harbour Bridge in Australia is a famous arch bridge. It uses cables suspended from a steel arch to hold up the road.

CANTILEVER BRIDGE

Cantilever bridges, like the Forth Bridge in Scotland, are built with sections that are only held up on one side, like a diving board.

BUILD YOUR OWN BRIDGE!

On the cover flaps of this book, there is a press-out model of a suspension bridge. Follow the instructions to press it out and build it.

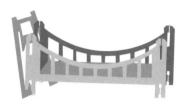

1. Press out all the pieces. Fold the two towers in half.

2. Fold up the sides of the bridge.

3. Slide the bottom of the bridge legs into the bottom notches of the towers.

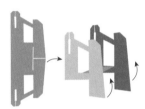

4. Gently push the top notches of the towers into the top notches of the bridge.

5. Fold up the sides of the end pieces.

6. Slide the end pieces up into the slots on the towers.

Once you have built your bridge, place your sticker here.

PLACE STICKER HERE

TASK COMPLETE

45

OFFICES

You might think offices are… well, a bit dull. You couldn't be more wrong! Millions of people all over the world work in **OFFICE BUILDINGS** and some of these buildings are amazing.

One of the most famous is **THE PENTAGON** in Washington, D.C. Back in 1942, approximately 15,000 people worked day and night to complete the massive headquarters for the United States Department of Defense.

It is a truly incredible achievement. For example:

- About **26,000 PEOPLE** work in The Pentagon.
- There are more than **SIX MILLION** square feet of floor space.
- Although there are 17 **MILES OF CORRIDORS** and 131 **STAIRCASES**, the clever design means that no two places in The Pentagon are more than a seven-minute walk apart.
- There are **284 TOILETS**.
- There is room for 8,770 **CARS** in the 16 **PARKING LOTS**.
- There are 16,250 **LIGHT FIXTURES**.
- The building has 7,754 **WINDOWS**.

There were a lot of very busy architects involved in the design. In fact, over **2,500 CONSTRUCTION DRAWINGS** were completed for the project

The Pentagon gets its name from its shape, because it is built in the shape of a pentagon (a five-sided figure). In fact, there are actually five pentagons, one inside the other and all linked together, as you can see in this aerial view of the building.

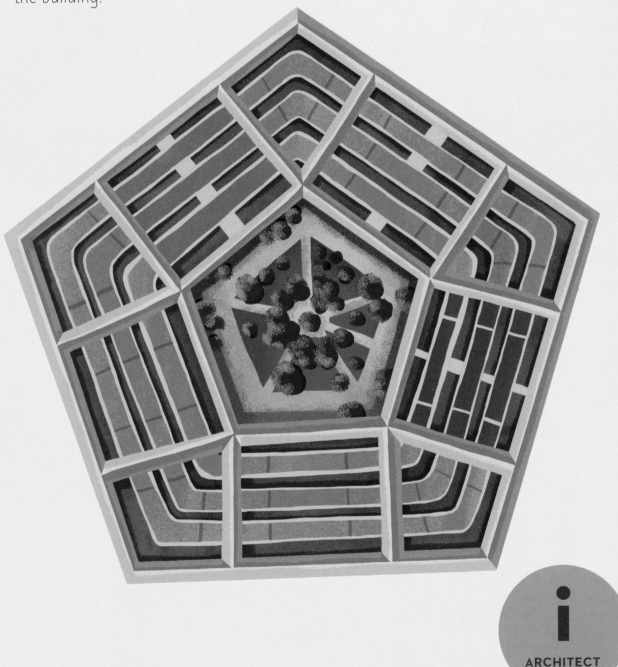

i

ARCHITECT
INFO

WEIRD AND WONDERFUL

As we have already seen, architects design all types of buildings, from homes and schools to theaters and libraries. Sometimes, they really let their imaginations run wild. Below, you can see some very creative designs.

This is the National Stadium in Beijing, China. It's not hard to see why it has been nicknamed "The Bird's Nest."

This incredible basket-shaped office building in Ohio is the headquarters of the Longaberger Basket Company.

The design of the Atomium in Brussels, Belgium, is based on an iron crystal, but is 165 billion times bigger!

The WonderWorks building in Tennessee was been designed to look like someone picked it up and then dropped it upside down.

The Crooked House in Poland is actually part of a shopping center.

It's difficult to ignore the Kansas City Public Library! The 20-foot-high "books" actually hide a parking area.

Congratulations! You are now a...

— QUALIFIED —
CONSTRUCTION EXPERT

NAME: -

The above-named architect
is qualified to be a

CONSTRUCTION EXPERT.

Architect Academy would like
to wish you every success in your
new career.

GOOD LUCK!

QUALIFICATION DATE: -

ECO ARCHITECTURE

Eco (or ecological) architects design buildings that use eco-friendly materials, such as paint that doesn't contain chemicals harmful to the environment. Buildings can even be constructed from recycled materials, such as car tires.

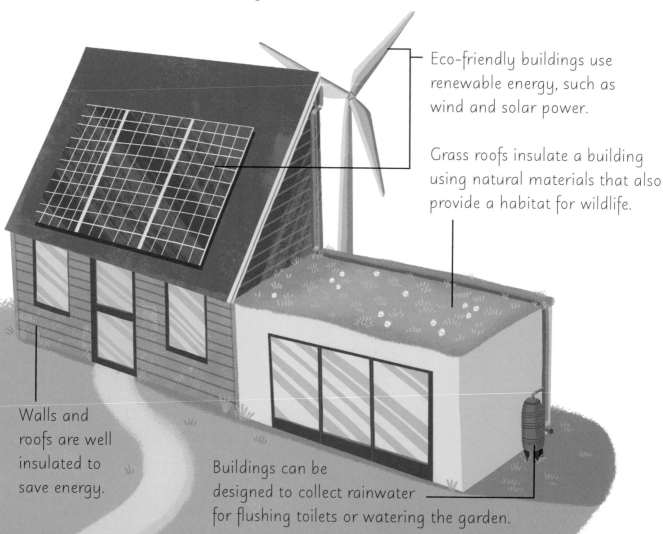

Eco-friendly buildings use renewable energy, such as wind and solar power.

Grass roofs insulate a building using natural materials that also provide a habitat for wildlife.

Walls and roofs are well insulated to save energy.

Buildings can be designed to collect rainwater for flushing toilets or watering the garden.

ENERGY-SAVING BOARD GAME

In this board game, the person who saves the most energy wins!

You will need: one die, 2 game pieces, a friend to play against

1. Take turns rolling the die and moving your game piece around the board.
2. If you land on a red circle, you have used up too much energy, so go back 4 spaces. If you land on a green circle, well done—you have saved energy! Move forward 4 spaces. The first person to reach the end wins.

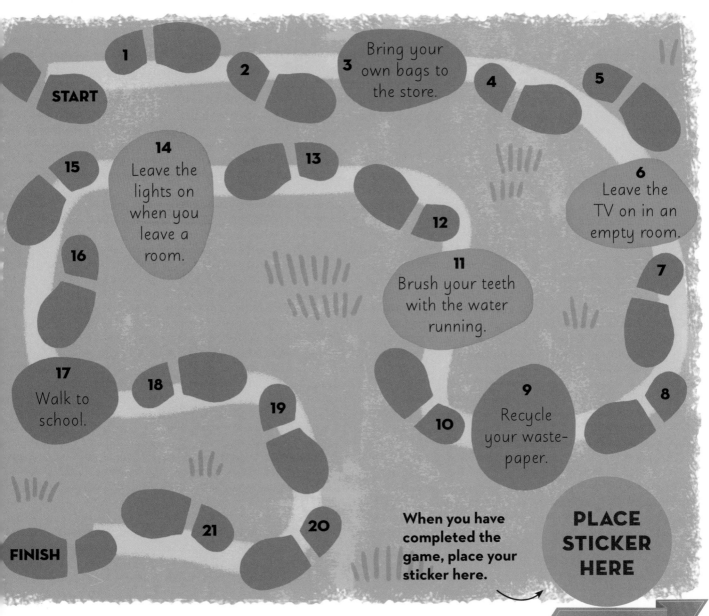

START

1 2 3 Bring your own bags to the store. 4 5

14 Leave the lights on when you leave a room. 13 12 6 Leave the TV on in an empty room.

15 16 11 Brush your teeth with the water running. 7

17 Walk to school. 18 19 9 Recycle your waste-paper. 10 8

FINISH 21 20

When you have completed the game, place your sticker here.

PLACE STICKER HERE

TASK COMPLETE

51

LANDSCAPE ARCHITECTURE

Landscape architects design all sorts of open spaces, including parks and gardens. They make these areas look appealing so that people enjoy visiting them, and usually also design them to protect wildlife and promote conservation.

FORMAL GARDENS

A formal garden uses straight lines, shapes and patterns. Often it will include hedges, neat pathways and flower beds laid out in patterns. It may also have statues and fountains, or trees and bushes trimmed into interesting shapes.

PARKS

Parks make the best use of the space available by including as much as possible while remaining green and attractive. A park might contain play areas, a skate park, cafés, lakes and areas to relax. There might even be themed areas, such as nature trails.

SEAFRONT

Families can spend all day at the beach so there should be plenty to do! There might be a boardwalk to stroll along, a wading pool for children, miniature golf, amusement arcades, a boating lake and ice cream stands.

MAZE CHALLENGE!

The twists and turns of hedge mazes have confused and entertained visitors to formal gardens for over 400 years. Find your way from the entrance of this maze to the center.

When you have found your way through the maze, collect your sticker and place it here.

PLACE STICKER HERE

TASK COMPLETE

A PERFECT PARK

PRACTICE YOUR LANDSCAPE ARCHITECT SKILLS

You are going to turn the empty space on the opposite page into the perfect park. Write down everything you want to include before you start, then think about how to fit it all in! Some ideas for what you might include are shown below, but use your own ideas as well.

PARK BENCH

POND

TENNIS COURT

PLAY AREA

BIKE PATH

FOUNTAIN

TREES AND BUSHES

ICE CREAM STAND

FLOWER BEDS

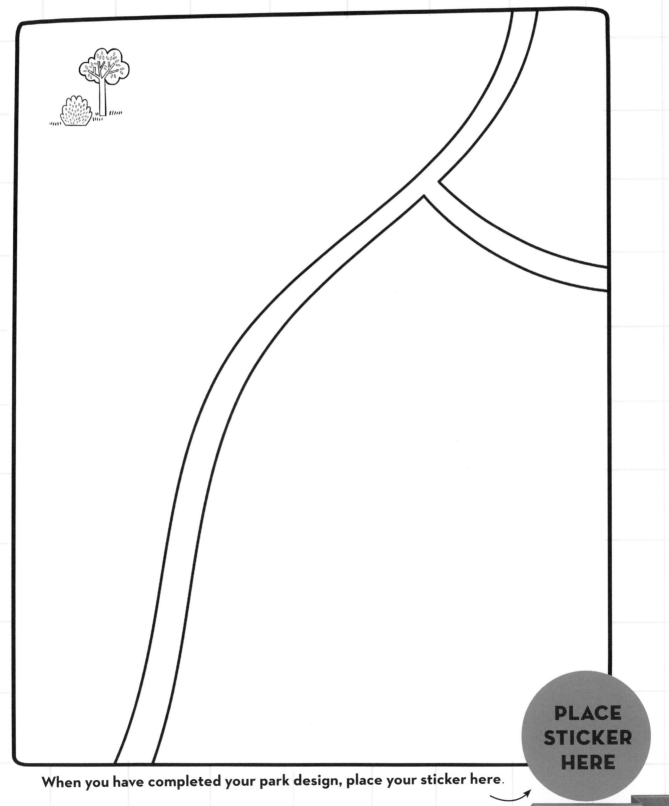

When you have completed your park design, place your sticker here.

NAVAL ARCHITECTURE

A naval architect designs all kinds of ships, from submarines to luxury cruise liners. Safety is the most important part of any ship design. Any vessel at sea needs to be stable enough to stay upright and strong enough to withstand the worst storms. Other design features will depend upon the type of ship and what it is used for.

FERRY
There is space for passengers and their cars, as well as ramps for cars to drive aboard quickly.

FISHING TRAWLER
Winches and ropes are used to haul nets full of fish aboard.

HOVERCRAFT
An air cushion underneath the craft allows it to glide across the water.

IDENTIFY THE DIFFERENT TYPES OF SHIP

You are now going to test your sea vessel recognition skills. Using the stickers at the back of the book, match each sticker to the correct craft.

CRUISE LINER
Hundreds of cabins, along with restaurants, theaters and swimming pools, allow vacationers to travel in style!

CONTAINER SHIP
Huge metal boxes (called containers) full of cargo are stacked on the long, flat deck.

AIRCRAFT CARRIER
An enormous wide, flat deck gives airplanes space to take off and land.

SUBMARINE
This vessel is shaped like a large, watertight tube so that it can travel underwater.

PLACE STICKER HERE

When you have matched all the ships, place your sticker here.

TASK COMPLETE

BOAT BUILDING

The most important part of any boat design is making sure it won't sink or tip over. You are about to test different designs to see which is the strongest and most stable.

BUILD AND TEST BOAT DESIGNS

You will need: several sheets of aluminum foil, a large bowl of water, pennies

1. Using the aluminum foil sheets, make each of the boat designs shown on the opposite page. You don't need any glue or tape—just press the foil into shape. If you like, you can try designing your own boat too.

2. Put each boat into the bowl of water and load it with pennies, counting them out one at a time until the boat sinks.

3. In the table opposite, record the number of coins each boat could hold before it sank. The more coins a boat can carry, the stronger and more stable it is. Which boat shape was the most stable?

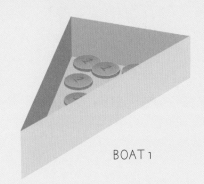

BOAT 1

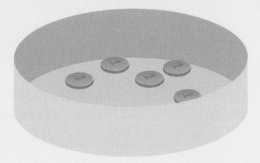

BOAT 2

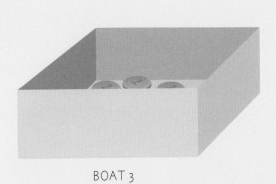

BOAT 3

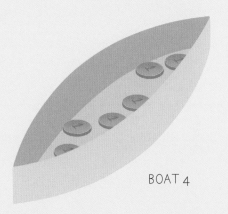

BOAT 4

	BOAT 1	BOAT 2	BOAT 3	BOAT 4
NUMBER OF COINS				

When you have tested your boats, place your sticker here.

PLACE STICKER HERE

TASK COMPLETE

INTERIOR DESIGN

Interior designers plan the insides of homes, stores, hotels, restaurants, offices and other buildings. They choose the style of the furniture and flooring, and decide which colors and types of fabric to use. Interior designers sometimes think of a theme for a room, and then use colors and patterns to match.

MATCH THE ITEMS TO THE THEMED ROOMS

Can you figure out which items belong in which bedroom on the opposite page? You can check your answers at the bottom of page 61.

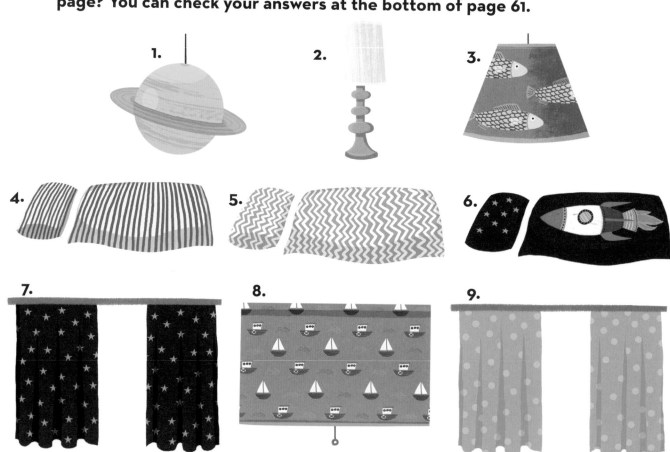

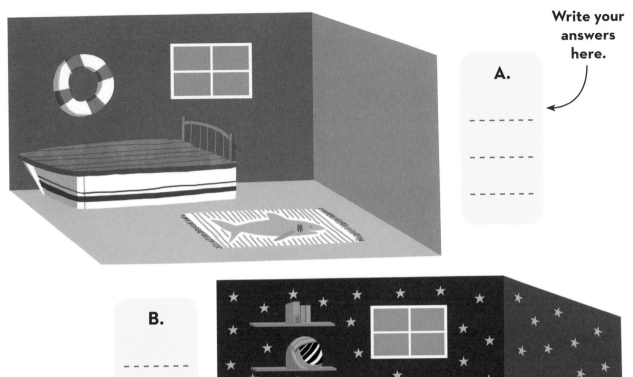

Write your answers here.

A.

- - - - - - -

- - - - - - -

- - - - - - -

B.

- - - - - - -

- - - - - - -

- - - - - - -

C.

- - - - - - -

- - - - - - -

- - - - - - -

When you have matched the items to the bedrooms, place your sticker here.

PLACE STICKER HERE

TASK COMPLETE

ANSWERS: Bedroom A: items 3, 4 and 8. Bedroom B: items 1, 6 and 7. Bedroom C: items 2, 5 and 9.

61

— QUALIFIED —
ARCHITECT SPECIALIST

NAME: -

The above-named architect
is qualified to be an

ARCHITECT SPECIALIST.

Architect Academy would like
to wish you every success in your
new career.

GOOD LUCK!

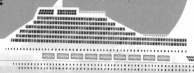

QUALIFICATION DATE: - - - - - - - - - - - - - - - - -

WELL DONE!

You have successfully completed all your tasks
and finished your architect training.

You are now ready to graduate from the Architect Academy.

**AS PART OF YOUR GRADUATION CEREMONY, YOU SHOULD READ
THE ARCHITECT'S CODE BELOW AND PROMISE TO FOLLOW IT.**

The Architect's Code

As an architect, I will be designing homes for people to live in and
important buildings that may be used for many years. In carrying
out my work, I promise that:

1. I will listen to my clients and do my best to
create the buildings they want and to spend
their money carefully.

2. All my buildings will be safe and I will build them
to meet all building rules.

3. I will continue to learn about buildings and architecture
so that I keep my skills and knowledge up-to-date.

4. I will work hard to design buildings that do
not harm the environment.

Draw or glue
a photo of your
face here.

Signed: _

ARCHITECT GOODIES!

IN THIS SECTION YOU WILL FIND LOTS OF GOODIES TO PLAY WITH:

- Pull-out architecture timeline poster

- Build It! board game

- Lots of fun stickers

- Bridge model (on the flaps of the book)

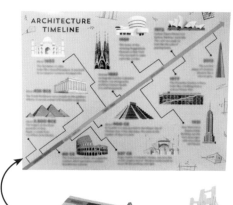

BUILD IT! GAME INSTRUCTIONS

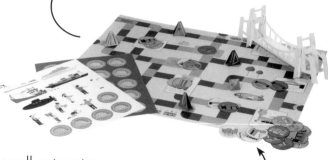

You'll find this game board on the reverse side of the pull-out poster.
Push out the die, then fold and glue it. Push out the game pieces and tokens.
Each player needs six tokens, one for each building on the board.

- **The object of the game is to land and leave a token on all six buildings. The first person to do this is the winner.**
- **Each player rolls a die and moves through the city streets in any direction.**
- **If a player chooses, he or she can move the game piece off the board into a tunnel and enter again through any other tunnel that enters or exits the city.**
- **When a player lands on a building, he or she places a token on it. The player then has to wait for his or her next turn to try to roll the number shown to construct the building.**
- **Once the player has rolled the correct number, he or she can move the game piece toward the next construction job. However, if a second player places a game piece on the same building while the first player is still there, the second player can remove the first player's game piece from the board and place it in any one of the tunnels around the city. This player has to wait until the next round to reenter the city.**
- **On the board there are three Advantage squares, which will help the players.**

BUILD IT TOKENS

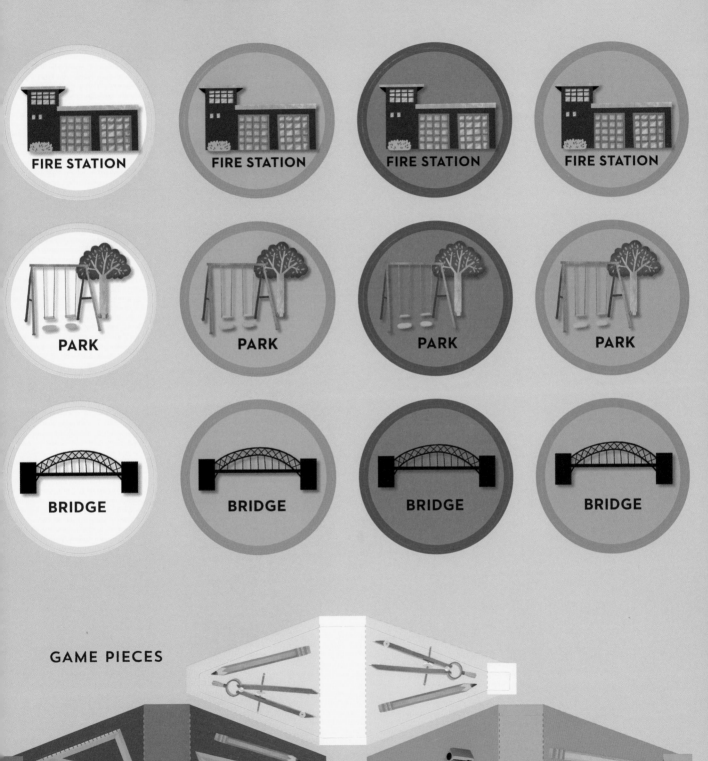

FIRE STATION   FIRE STATION   FIRE STATION   FIRE STATION

PARK   PARK   PARK   PARK

BRIDGE   BRIDGE   BRIDGE   BRIDGE

GAME PIECES

BUILD IT TOKENS

MUSEUM   MUSEUM   MUSEUM   MUSEUM

APARTMENT BUILDING   APARTMENT BUILDING   APARTMENT BUILDING   APARTMENT BUILDING

AIRPORT   AIRPORT   AIRPORT   AIRPORT

DIE   GAME PIECE

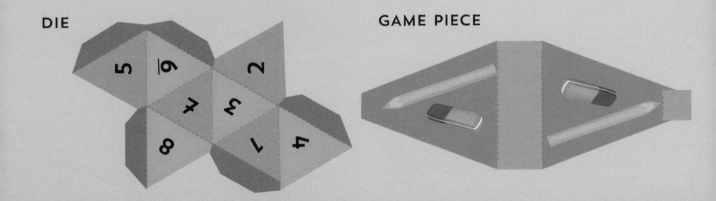

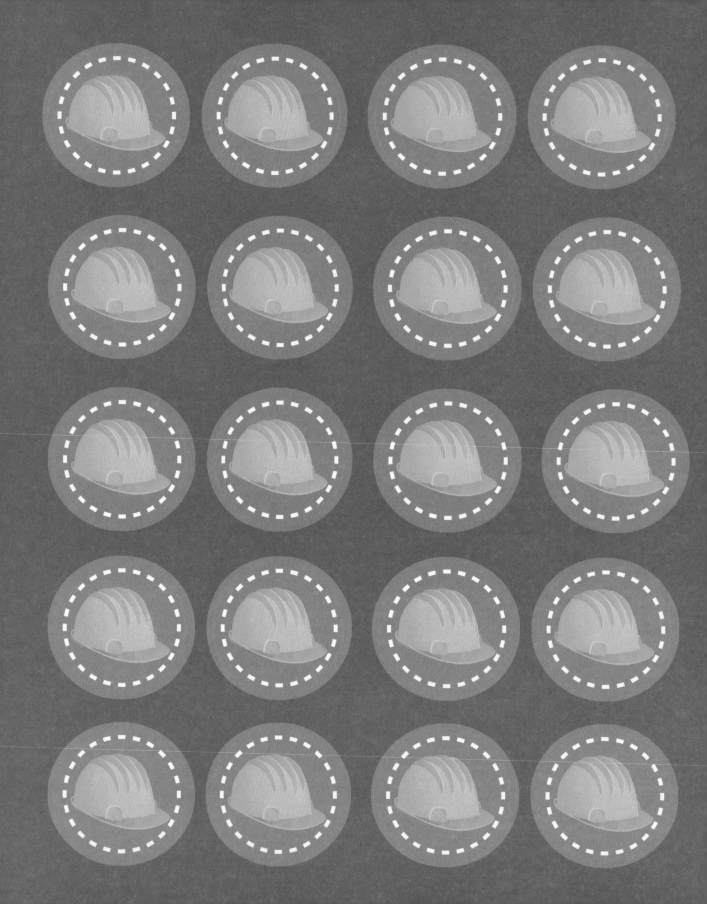